PRAISE FOR *THE MILLE...*

"It's like John Stewart meets Kanye meets Adele"

"This will make even Grumpy Cat smile!"

"First I'm going to do something for the environment, then I'm going to read this book and reinvent laughter."

"I'm going to give this to all my friends, I will never have to go on Twitter again."

"There is not an emoticon which can capture the feelings this book creates."

"The emoticon for this book is a gigantic eagle carrying someone to the top of Mt. Laugh-Out-Loud."

The Millennial Joke Book

Ken Habarta and Sally Forth

Copyright © 2014 Ken Habarta

All rights reserved.

ISBN: 0615994997
ISBN-13: 978-0615994994

DEDICATION

This book is dedicated to the entire global Millennial population – all 95 Million of them. This even includes the 35 Million who are still living at home with their parents.

ACKNOWLEDGMENTS

This book was made by Millennials for Millennials. Or more accurately, I got much needed help and motivation from my essential Millennial conspirators. Metta-world peace-fully proving this generation has a great sense of humor – and can be a real source of inspiration. And they are getting a cut of whatever little money this book makes, unless this number is so small that it negates splitting. They also pointed out the jokes initially were not very funny. Not even conceptually. Whether this misses the point or not, thank you for sharing.

329-WORD FOREWORD

What truly defines a generation? Timelines and young people. I wish I was present at the birth of generational analysis, when those brilliant and prescient marketing nerds were first embarking on work that would not only revolutionize market research but would in fact transform our society. By the time they had labeled those early generations, who could resist the allure of those exciting new pre-packaged identities, and who could argue against the case for falling in line and assuming one's place among the rank-and-file of one's cohort?

America needed the vocabulary to discuss and comprehend the phenomenon that we now readily identify as the Boomers. Thanks to generational analysis, comprehension had indeed become possible. Vast, unexpected sociocultural shifts that seemed inconceivable and incomprehensible now had in the Boomers a clear, straightforward, and ready explanation. The Boomers changed the world, the generational analysis helped America process this change, and we, the Millennial generation, were less than a twinkle in America's sociocultural eye.

When the Millennials, my cohort, arrived, the country was ready – ready to watch our emergence and our rise. After the false start that was and, sadly, remains Generation X, market research was ready – for the first time, ready – to take on this new generation that would take on the world. With the exceptional as the founding charter, we the Millennials have had the eyes of the generational world upon us from the beginning.

And we have grown. With our ascent, we claim from the Boomers the mantle of generational greatness that is our birthright, and we bask in the satisfaction of our success, renderers of a society's dreams fulfilled. That we are bright, shining stars, each of us, has become an inescapable truth. Collectively, our light is so bright that only the blindness that it induces in those who stare too hard can diminish our brilliance.

But don't be deterred – I urge you to stare on, lest you miss out. You only live once.

INTRODUCTION

The Millennial Joke Book is the first joke book of its kind to put an entire generation in the comedy crosshairs. Also known as Generation Y, the Millennials — people born between 1979 and 1996 – are the natural target here. Just as important are the marketers dreaming up these labels in the first place and propagating the myth of the Millennial. They. Of the eternal mixed reviews. Basically this joke book is one giant cultural feedback loop aimed at generational stereotypes and Generational Marketing. While there were some efforts to make this funny, there was not a pressure to BE funny. This is a conceptual joke book after all, not a joke book in the classic sense. Pointing that out makes me a little sad, but if you happen to find some of this funny then consider it a magic prize at the bottom of the cereal box. A comedy gift which keeps giving, like the Millennial cohort itself.

Also, there were no Millennials harmed in the making of this book. This is a generation who is very open to humor at their expense – more so than any generation preceding them. They are tuned-in to their behavior and personalities. They seem to like poking fun at themselves…in that self-referential-post-modern-I'm-making-the-joke-you-should-have-were-you-clever-enough-to-have-thought-of-it-yourself. They seem to not mind the blowhards wasting away time analyzing them instead of doing something tangible in the world. Well I sincerely hope this book gets us past that.

The Millennial Joke Book

Why did the Millennial cross the road?

Everyone gets a trophy for road-crossing.

How many Millennials does it take to screw in a lightbulb?

None, their parents screw it in.

How many Millennials does it take to screw in a lightbulb?

Four. One to screw it in, one to tweet about it, one to instagram it, and one to create a "screwing in lightbulbs" tumblr.

Why are Millennials so optimistic?

Xanax.

Why did the Millennial fail at being a ghost?

He stopped believing in himself.

Why are suicide rates so low for Millennials?

Because they haven't figured out how they can check-in from the afterlife (yet).

What do you call a Millennial that is left-handed?

Gifted and Talented.

How tall is the average Millennial?

They are not average.

What do you call a fat Millennial?

Someone who insists you see them for their intelligence.

What is the best gift for a Millennial?

A mirror which tweets its reflection back to them.

How do you boost a Millennial's confidence?

Use a sepia-toned Instagram filter.

Two cannibals are eating a Millennial and the one says, "Millennials make the best barbeque -- they're so self involved they soak in their own juices."

What do you get when you cross a Millennial with a Vampire?

Someone who is devastated by not seeing their reflection in the mirror.

How do you kill a Millennial Vampire?

With an hand-carved Mahogany stake.

What do you get when you cross a Millennial with The Godfather?

An offer which doesn't interfere with their personal life.

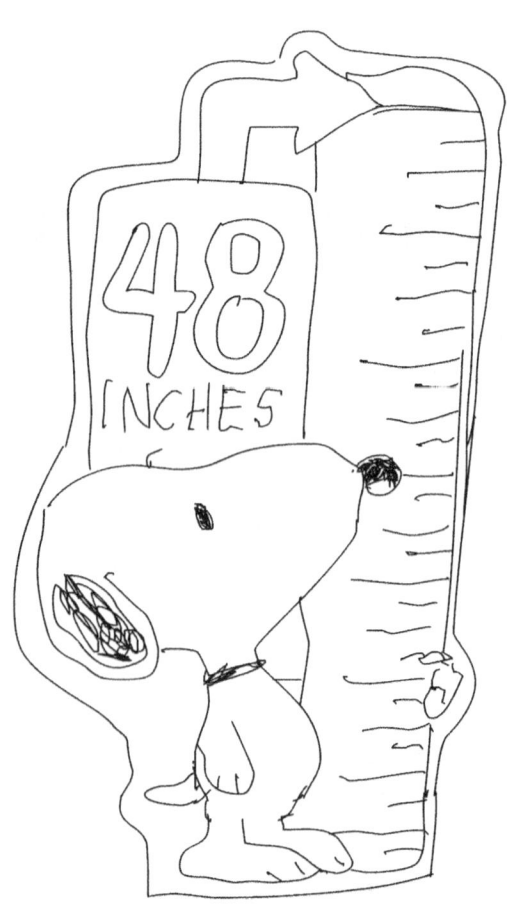

What kind of toilet paper do Millennials use?

Anything which provides a boost to their confidence.

What rides do Millennials enjoy at theme parks?

None, they won't go on anything with height restrictions. They all know someone short.

Why do Millennials like working from home?

Because their parents tell them everything they do is wonderful.

Why is it so hard to be a Millennial?

Staying hydrated and being healthy takes a lot of work.

Why did the Millennial get a trophy?

Everyone gets a trophy.

A Millennial, after many years in prison, is finally released. He runs around yelling, "I'm free! I'm free!"

A post-Millennial walks up to him and says, "So what, I'm 4."

How do you stop a Millennial from dancing?

Why would you want them to stop?

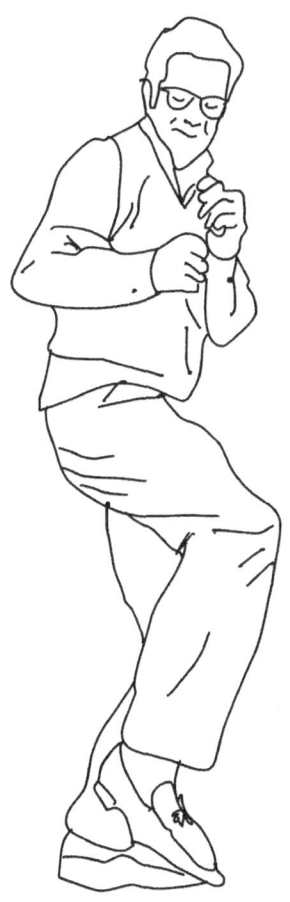

Knock Knock

Who's there?

Wait, do you want my ironic self or the profile my extended family sees?

Knock Knock

Who's there?

A Millennial coming for your job.

How can Millennials improve their credit score?

Grade them on a curve.

What does a Millennial and a bicycle seat have in common?

They are both under enormous debt.

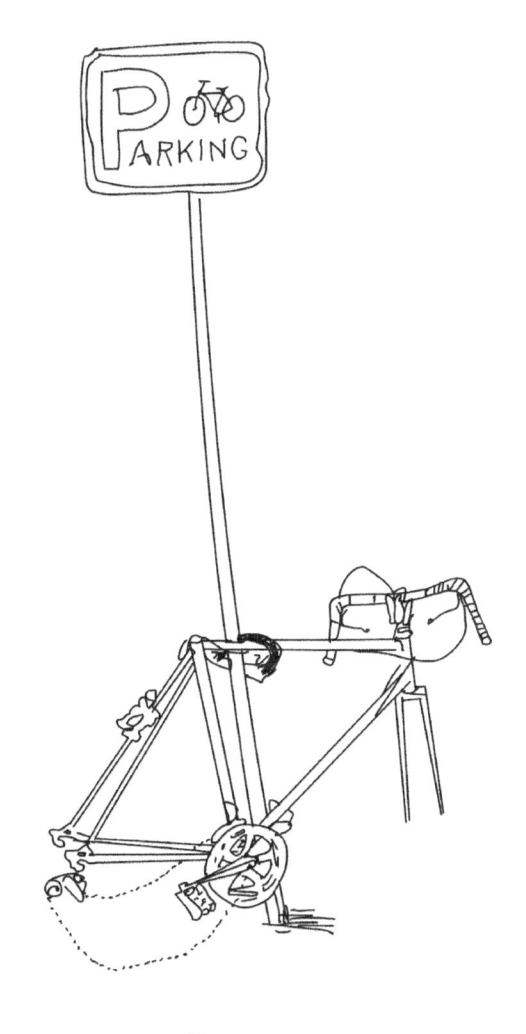

Why did the Millennial go to the expensive college?

What do Millennials do when they are horny?

They get focussed on their careers.

What are Millennials preferred contraceptives?

Commitment.

What did one gay Millennial say to the other?

Are you still living at home with your parents?

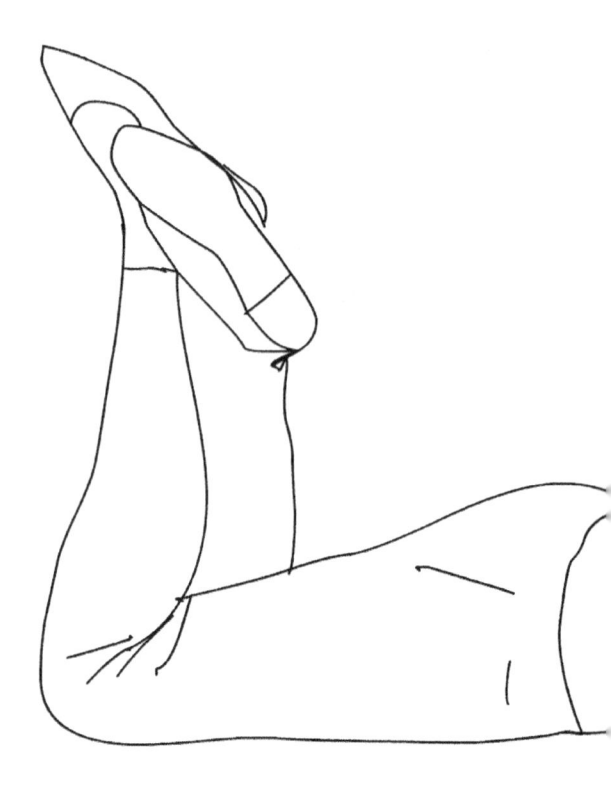

What do you get when you put 50 Millennials in a room with 50 Gen Xers?

Mutual disdain.

God is not dead, he's trapped in a cycle of internships with little pay and no job offers.

What did the Millennial say when her doctor told her that she was pregnant?

Can I get the wifi password for this office?

What happened to the special, unique one-of-a-kind snowflake?

Its parents sent it to college, it started a blog and it melted.

A Millennial walks into a bar and orders a PBR.

THIS IS YOUR FAULT

A Rabbi, and a Holocaust survivor and a Millennial walk into a bar.
They bartender asks, whaddya have?

The Rabbi says, "If it's not too much trouble, I'll take a manischewitz."

The Holocaust survivor says, "I would be more than grateful for even a glass a water."

The Millennial says, "Am I in a meme?"

How do you get a Millennial to stop watching TV?

You make them pay for it.

Why didn't the Millennial text and drive?

They didn't own a car.

What is better than being hit by a car?

Being hit by a Prius.

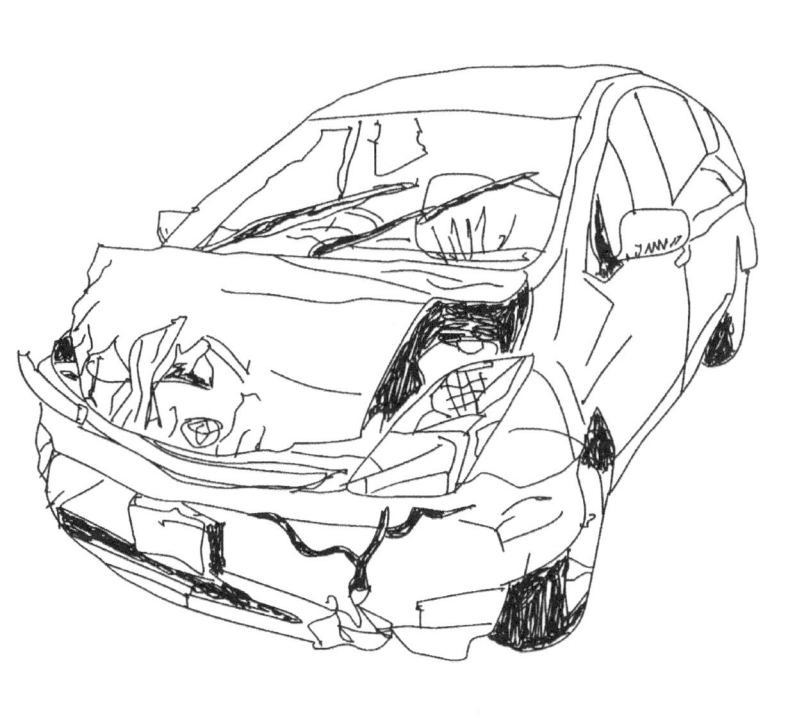

A Millennial walks into a bar with their parents.

The bartender says, "Hey we don't serve Millennials here."

What did the Millennial get for Christmas?

All the GIFs he ever wanted.

Why did the Millennial couple get a divorce?

The marriage was no longer what they wanted it to be.

Did you hear about the Millennial 10K race?

Everybody got first place for just tweeting about it.

Why are ebooks not popular gifts with Millennials?

You can't wrap an ebook in recycled paper.

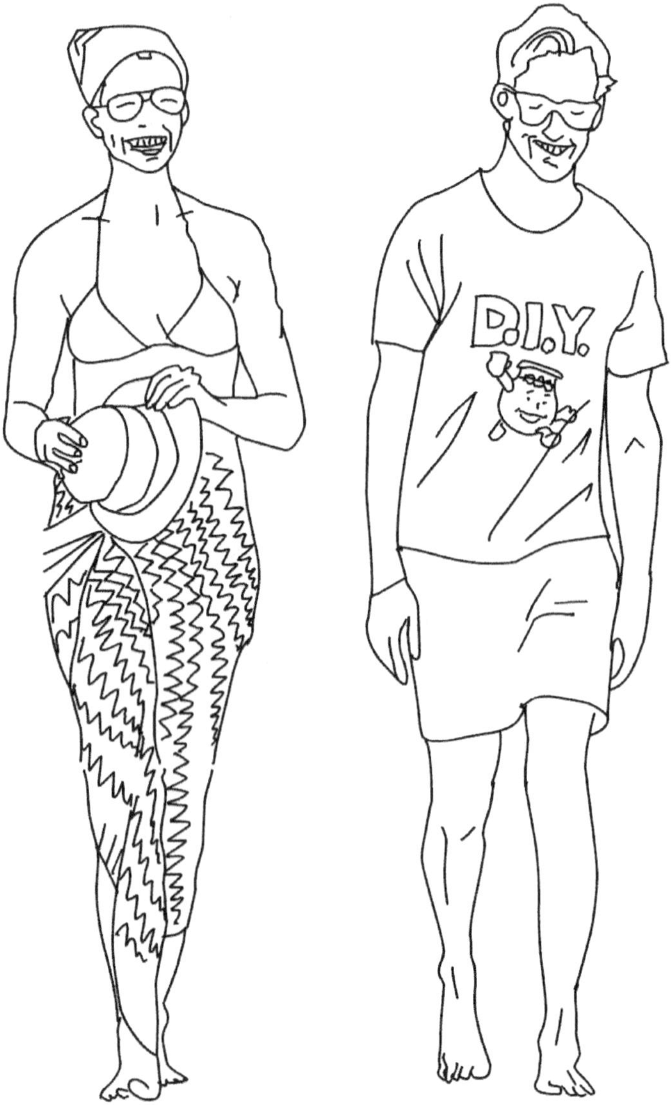
D.I.Y.

Why did the Millennial wear a swim suit in a blizzard?

She was dressing for the weather she wanted and not the weather she had.

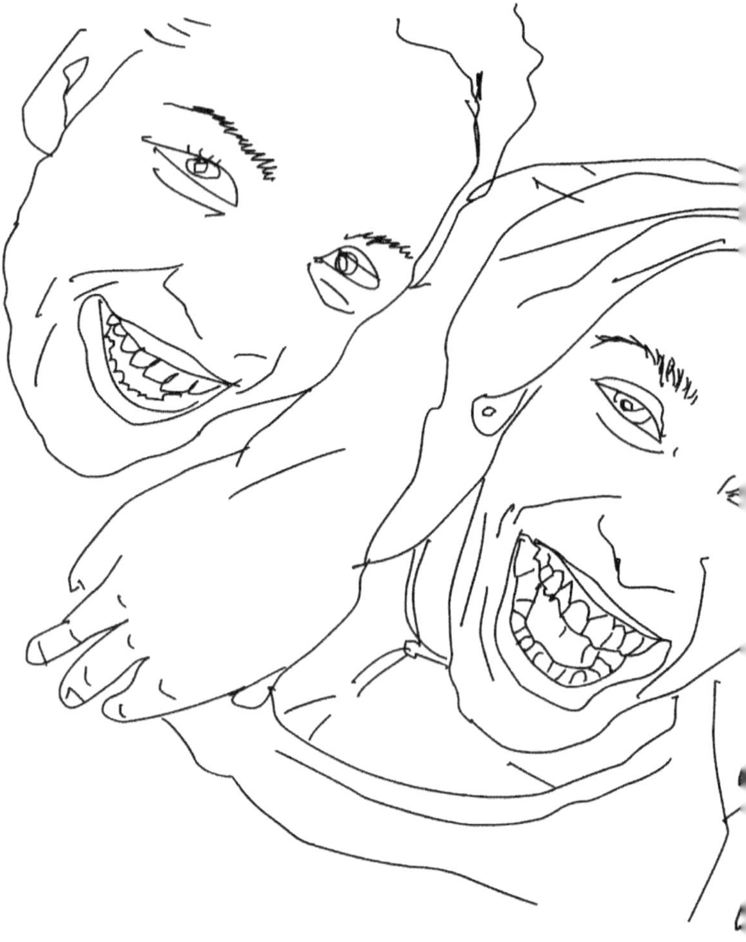

What do you call a Millennial in the Emergency Room?

Impatient.

What happened when the Millennial walked into the bar?

They wrote a scathing review on Yelp.

A Millennial walks into a bar, orders four shots of the most artisan, locally-sourced whisky, and downs them one after the other.

The barkeep says, "You look like you're in a hurry."

"You would be too if you had what I have," says the Millennial.

"What have you got?" asks the barkeep.

"ADHD."

What do Millennials like to eat for breakfast?

Constant Feedback Loops.

What washed up on the beach during a Millennial vacation?

Debris from the latest hurricane caused by climate change.

Why do Millennials not give to the homeless?

The homeless app is glitchy.

Why did the Millennial have a hard time getting into the hotel?

He didn't understand the meaning of "no."

Did you hear about the new paint for Millennials?

It's flame retardant.

What happens when a Millennial sets themselves on fire?

They feel the burn.

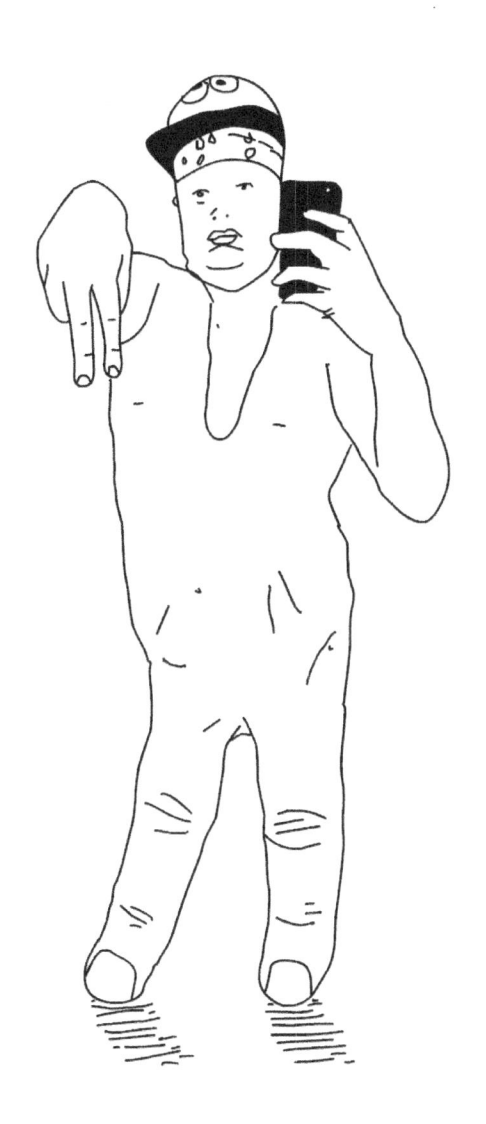

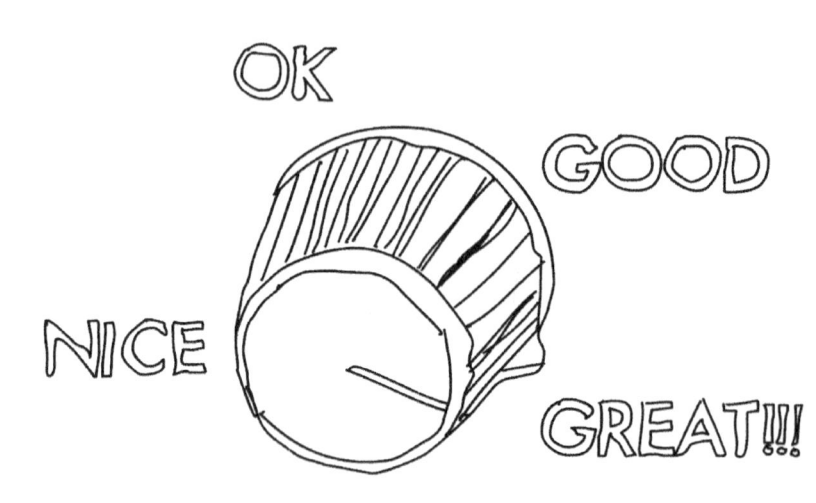

What did the Millennial guitarist say to the singer of the band?

I need more feedback.

Why was 6 mad at 7?

Because 7 was "just being honest" with 6.

What did the Millennial want more than a delicious meal?

A photo of it.

Why did the Millennial take their smartphone to the doctor?

It had lost its APPetite for taking pictures of food.

ABOUT THE AUTHORS

Ken Habarta was born in 1970, a Generation Xer. For some this may not be surprising given the snarky and ironic tone of this book. When he was younger and Millennial-aged he had a vision, or rather lots of smaller visions which comprised one super vision. One which would take an entire generation to realize. He just had to wait until the youth of the 90s got a little bit older, developed more of a sense of humor. Part of the blame for this book comes from a decade's work as a consultant to the marketing industry. He previously published Bank Notes – a collection of hand-written notes used in bank robberies. He lives in New York with his wife and two children.

Sally Forth doesn't like the idea of writing a bio one bit. It feels too restraining and one-dimensional. She has enjoyed working on this project with Ken, whose humor left much to be desired -- but which also made her turns of phrase that much more impressive! She hopes you enjoy this book, but also thinks you should go pick up "A Prairie Home Companion Pretty Good Joke Book" if you're looking for real knee slappers.

Made in United States
North Haven, CT
16 December 2023